Big Bad Buzz

Written by Charnan Simon • Illustrated by Len Esptein

Published in the United States of America by The Child's World®
PO Box 326 • Chanhassen, MN 55317-0326
800-599-READ • www.childsworld.com

Reading Adviser

Cecilia Minden-Cupp, PhD, Former Language and Literacy Program Director,
Harvard Graduate School of Education, Cambridge, Massachusetts

Acknowledgments

The Child's World®: Mary Berendes, Publishing Director

Editorial Directions, Inc.: E. Russell Primm, Editorial Director and Project Manager;
Katie Marsico, Associate Editor; Judith Shiffer, Assistant Editor; Caroline Wood, Editorial Assistant

The Design Lab: Kathleen Petelinsek, Design and Art Production

Library of Congress Cataloging-in-Publication Data

Simon, Charnan.
    Big bad Buzz / written by Charnan Simon ; illustrated by Len Epstein.
      p. cm. — (Magic door to learning)
    Summary: Shauna learns a lesson in bravery when she visits her cousin Lucy and faces big
bad Buzz the dog.
    ISBN 1-59296-617-9 (library bound : alk. paper)
    [1. Courage—Fiction. 2. Dogs—Fiction.]   I. Epstein, Len, ill.   II. Title. III. Series.
PZ7.S6035Big 2006
    [E]—dc22   2006001404

A book is a door, a magic door.

It can take you places

you have never been before.

Ready? Set?

Turn the page.

Open the door.

Now it is time to explore.

Shauna loved everything
about visiting Cousin
Lucy, except Lucy's dog
Buzz. "Keep that big
bad Buzz away from
me!" she said.

"Oh, pooh!" said Lucy.
"Buzz is just a sweetie-pie!"

She then gave Buzz a kiss
on his big bad head.

Shauna shuddered.
"All those teeth!" she
said. "Let's play with
Shadow instead!"

9

Shadow was Lucy's kitten. No
one could be afraid of such a
soft, furry, purry little cat!

The next morning,
Shauna heard a noise
upstairs. It was a sad,
scared, whiney noise.

14

Shauna went to the hall.
There was Buzz, whining
at the top of the stairs.
There was Shadow, purring
halfway up the stairs.

Buzz saw Shauna. He wagged
his tail and started down the stairs.

16

Swipe! Shadow's paw smacked
big bad Buzz right on the nose.

Buzz scooted back up
the stairs. He stopped
wagging his tail. He
looked at Shauna with
sad eyes. He whined.

19

"Shadow," said Shauna, "You are not such a soft, furry, purry little cat after all!"

20

"Buzz," said Shauna, "You may be big,
but you are not very mean."

Shauna took a deep
breath. She picked up
Shadow and sat down
next to Buzz. "Be nice!"
she said to Shadow. "I'll
keep you safe," she said to
Buzz. "You big scaredy-cat
sweetie-pie!"

Our story is over, but there is still much to explore beyond the magic door!

People own many different kinds of pets besides cats and dogs. Some people own unusual pets such as snakes, hedgehogs, or potbellied pigs! Visit your local pet store and ask what is involved in taking care of one of these pets. Find out if the animal is easy or difficult to care for, what it eats, where it lives, and if it is friendly. If you still want to know more, check out some books from the library and talk to your family veterinarian.

These books will help you explore at the library and at home:

Clements, Andrew. *Brave Norman: A True Story.* New York: Simon & Schuster Books for Young Readers, 2001.
Cocca-Leffler, Maryann. *Bravery Soup.* Morton Grove, Ill.: A. Whitman, 2002.
Stohner, Anu. *Brave Charlotte.* New York: Bloomsbury Children's Books, 2005.

About the Author

Charnan Simon lives in Madison, Wisconsin, where she can usually be found sitting at her desk and writing books, unless she is sitting at her desk and looking out the window. Charnan has one husband, two daughters, and two very helpful cats.

About the Illustrator

Len Epstein is living a dream . . . he loves to draw and draw and draw! When he's not drawing, Len enjoys being more immature than his grandchildren. His studio is in Narberth, Pennsylvania.